April in July

KEITH ALJREW

Copyright © 2019 by Keith Aljrew

All rights reserved. No part of this book may be used or reproduced by any means, graphic, electronic, or mechanical, including photocopying, recording, taping, or by any information storage retrieval system, without the written permission of the publisher except in the case of brief quotations embodied in critical articles and reviews.

Dedication

To Those Who Still Believe In Santa!

Table of Contents

Catharsis 1
Red Wine 2
Sweet Nectar 3
White Sheets 4
Wrong 5
Hell 6
Cigarette 7
Language Barrier 8
April in July 9
Memory Issues! 11
I Miss Her 12
Fair Trade 13
Memories 14
Eclipse 15
A Side Talk on The Sidewalk 16
Virgin 17
Lust and Love 18
Scared! 19
Words 20
Tell Me I'm Beautiful! 21

Catharsis

feelings captured
words sentenced
soul set free!

Red Wine

her lips were my wine of choice
one sip and i was lost
with each kiss
i felt thirst
for more!
so i kept kissing her,
the sweet taste of red wine...

Sweet Nectar

we didn't kiss...
our lips danced with one another,
like two bees
searching for sweet nectar.

White Sheets

under the white sheets,
she lays naked.
her beautiful body flows,
endless, peaceful, flawless!
her long black hair spans over her shoulders and white pillowcases,
her lips bright pink.
morning dew rests,
bronze sunrays brush across the white curtains,
mist of the night vapors,
then, suddenly, her eyes open!
and a soft smile breaks through her lips,
"good morning!"

Wrong

"it's wrong,"
she whispered faintly.
but it feels right!
i replied as i pushed her frail body against the wall...
let's do the one wrong that makes us feel right!
feel alive!
fire erupts...
script goes ablaze!
poem lost,
moment gained!

Hell

hell is my heaven
if you're in it
with me!

Cigarette

thin white smoke,
smoking high,
slowly burning,
red wine...
scent of bad habits,
lonely souls,
colliding through ether.

Language Barrier

we didn't speak each other's language...
"let's stop talking!"
i wrote.
let's see if our lips can finish what our tongues have started!
without words being spoken!
we then talked and talked...
more than words could have ever said!

April in July

i've made a mistake,
i've stared into her eyes!
i'm no longer mad at her,
i'm mad at myself!
flashbacks!
the tales are true!
she can hear my thoughts,
she can seize my soul!
"run! run!"
my brain pleaded!
but i sat still,
in awe of what i saw...

i kneeled

at the edge of her throne

my lips muttered:

"i'm sorry, my queen!"

"here's my heart!"

"do with it as you wish"

"after all, it only beats for you!"

...silence...

stars fall...

the sun rises...

golden rays wash over his headstone,

it reads:

"he saw her heaven

and died a happy man!

at peace,

at last."

april, 26th, 2018

Memory Issues!

i forgot what i was about to say,
i forgot what i was trying to do,
i forgot not to stare!
i forgot to care...
who's watching and who's there!
i forgot that i forgot!

i closed my eyes,
in utter despair...
suddenly...
i remember everything!
her hair,
her eyes,
her nose,
her lips,
her neck,
her hands,
her feet,
her voice,
her scent!
if her memory was my last,
i'd die a happy man!

I Miss Her

i miss her
but my ego would never let me tell her...
how much i miss her.

i see her figure runs through the corridor,
her black hair caressing the air.

i go to her room,
to catch her scent,
i linger,
to breathe it in,
for air is life,
life's beat.
then,
i hear her voice
and the animal within me awakens.
so i run out the room to protect her,
before i have my fill,
damn you, me!
you're killing me!

Fair Trade

i said,

"take my heart and i will give you the whole wide world!"

she replied,

"nah!"

Memories

do you still think of her?
or do you even remember her?
how could you remember someone you never forgot?
so you miss her?
but how could you miss someone you never really got to know?
so you want to see her again?
yes!!!

Eclipse

"do not look at the sun!" they warned.
"you will go blind," they said.
well, i did and i have.
i've stared at the sun with my bare eyes.
and since then i've gone blind.
for all i could see is her light,
and all the rest is but a dark night!
regrets, i have none.
her shine will forever be my last sight!

A Side Talk on The Sidewalk

we ran into each other.
we haven't talked since that last text i sent.
over a year ago.
"hi keith!" she said with her familiar voice.
my heart tripped.
words jammed at my lips and my eyes stood still.
they were trying to take her in,
all of her…
that moment lasted just enough for me to calm my heart,
when my stupid ego took over.
the lights said: walk! so i walked away!
"see you later,"
were the last words i heard her say.
those were the sweetest, bitterest words i've ever heard.

Virgin

I'm still a virgin!
What?! You've never had sex before?!
No, I've never made love!

Lust and Love

others get my lust.

she gets my love,

lust and everything else i have!

Scared!

she said, "keith, you scared me!"
she did not know i was the one scared!
you sneaked up on my heart
and showed up at its door,
unannounced,
and uninvited!
but i don't hate her,
i don't love her either,
i don't know what to make of you!

Words

"what are you offering?" she asked.
my heart, he muttered,
... and my words!

Tell Me I'm Beautiful!

he looked up...
his eyes ravenous for everything she is!
yet he said nothing...
his mind was starved...
for words...
"tell me i'm beautiful!" she demanded.
but...
"but what?" she asked.
her voice was eager mixed with anger and gin!
"but you're a lot more than...
just...
beautiful!"

www.ingramcontent.com/pod-product-compliance
Lightning Source LLC
LaVergne TN
LVHW051513070426
835507LV00022B/3090